LIBRARY SE

D0310958

President Kennedy School Library
13936

World in Focus
Egypt

JEN GREEN

WAYLAND

First published in 2006 by Wayland,
an imprint of Hachette Children's Books

Copyright © Wayland 2006

All rights reserved. Apart from any use permitted under UK copyright
law, this publication may only be reproduced, stored or transmitted, in
any form, or by any means with prior permission in writing of the
publishers or in the case of reprographic production in accordance with
the terms of licences issued by the Copyright Licensing Agency.

Hachette Children's Books
338 Euston Road, London NW1 3BH

Commissioning editor: Nicola Edwards
Editor: Patience Coster
Inside design: Chris Halls, www.mindseyedesign.co.uk
Cover design: Hodder Wayland
Series concept and project management by EASI-Educational Resourcing
(info@easi-er.co.uk)
Statistical research: Anna Bowden
Maps and graphs: Martin Darlison, Encompass Graphics

British Library Cataloguing in Publication Data
Green, Jen
    Egypt. - (World in focus)
    1. Egypt - Juvenile literature
    I. Title
    962'.055

ISBN-10: 0750247398
ISBN-13: 978-0-75024-739-9

Printed and bound in China

COVENTRY SCHOOLS LIBRARY SERVICE	
	J916.2
PETERS	

Cover top: The Sphinx at Giza, among the best known sights of Egypt.
Cover bottom: Egyptian craft called feluccas have been seen on the Nile since the time of the pharaohs.
Title page: The pyramids at Giza, considered one of the Seven Wonders of the World in ancient times.

The author and publisher would like to thank the following for allowing their pictures to be reproduced in
this publication:
Corbis 8 (Christine Osborne), 9 (Khaled El-Fiqi/epa), 10 (Leonard de Selva), 11 (Hulton-Deutsch Collection), 12
(Bettmann), 13 (Kevin Fleming), 14 , 23 (National Democratic Party/Handout/Reuters), 24 (Tara Whitehill/Reuters), 25
(Shawn Baldwin), 26 (Paul Dowd/Eye Ubiquitous), 34 (Bobby Yip/Reuters), 35 (David Rubinger), 36 (Khaled El-Fiqi/epa),
37 (Frederic Neema/Corbis Sygma), 43 (Thomas Hartwell), 45 (Aladin Abdel Naby/Reuters), 48 (Christine Osborne), 49
(Thomas Hartwell), 56 (The Cover Story), 57 (David A. Northcott), 59 (Bojan Brecelj/Corbis Sygma); EASI-Images (Rob
Bowden) cover (top) and 5, 16, 18, 52; EASI-Images (Roy Maconachie) cover (bottom), title page and 46, 4, 6, 15, 17, 19, 20,
21, 22, 27, 28, 29, 30, 31, 32, 33, 38, 39, 40, 41, 42, 44, 47, 50, 51, 53, 54, 55, 58.

The website addresses (URLs) included in this book were valid at the time of going to press. However, because of the
nature of the Internet, it is possible that some addresses may have changed, or sites may have changed or closed down
since publication. While the author and publishers regret any inconvenience this may cause the readers, no responsibility
for any such changes can be accepted by either the author or the publisher.

The directional arrow portrayed on the map on page 7 provides only an approximation of north.

The data used to produce the graphics and data panels in this title were the latest available at the time of production.

CONTENTS

CHAPTER 1

Egypt – An Overview

Egypt is an Arab nation situated in the north-east corner of Africa. The important role Egypt plays in international politics may at first seem out of keeping with its size and wealth. Although it is a large country, it is neither a geographic nor an economic giant. Egypt owes part of its importance to its location, forming a land bridge between Africa and Asia. The Suez Canal, which runs through Egypt, provides a link between the Mediterranean Sea, Arabian Sea and Indian Ocean. This waterway is of major importance in transporting vital supplies such as oil. Egypt is also famous for its ancient civilization and antiquities.

Egypt consists mainly of a squarish landmass in north-east Africa, plus a smaller triangle of land to the east, the Sinai Peninsula, which is geographically part of Asia. It is bounded by the Mediterranean Sea to the north, Libya to the west and Sudan to the south. It is also flanked by Israel, the Gaza Strip that borders the Mediterranean, and the Red Sea to the east. Much of Egypt is occupied by a high desert plateau, which is very sparsely populated.

▼ Modern buildings rise not far from the slender towers, known as minarets, of the Sultan Hassan and El Rifai mosques in Cairo.

The River Nile runs north through the desert, producing a narrow strip of fertile farmland. In ancient times, the Greek writer Herodotus wrote, 'Egypt is the gift of the Nile'. Almost all of the country's population lives along the river and its marshy delta to the north.

A LONG HISTORY

Egypt is a land of contradictions: at once an ancient country and also a young one that has only existed since the 1950s. Some 7,000 years ago, one of the world's most advanced civilizations developed on the banks of the Nile. Ruled by kings called pharaohs, the ancient Egyptians were expert astronomers, skilful artists and master builders. The huge size and architectural precision of monuments such as the pyramids are still astounding. From the first millennium BC, Egypt was conquered by a series of foreign powers, including the Greeks, Romans, Arabs, Turks and lastly the British (from the 1880s). Egypt only became independent in 1952 (see page 12).

Egypt has been an Arabic republic since the 1950s. It defines itself as a democracy but, in practice, its form of democracy is limited. Since independence, almost all power in Egypt has been concentrated in the hands of the president, and political opposition has largely been denied a voice. In 2005, Egypt claimed to hold its first free elections, but opposition to the ruling National Democratic Party was still restricted. Many commentators consider that Egypt's president holds sovereign power comparable to that of the pharaohs of ancient times.

▶ The enigmatic figure of the Sphinx at Giza is among the best known sights of Egypt. This guardian statue, with the body of a lion and a human head, is known as the 'Father of Terrors' in Arabic.

ECONOMICS AND POLITICS

In 2005, Egypt's population was the second largest in Africa after Nigeria, and the largest in the Arab world. Egypt is one of the world's fastest-growing nations, with a third of the population under the age of 15. It is a poor country compared with developed nations such as the USA and UK. Since the 1960s, reforms have encouraged economic growth, but ambitious development projects begun around the same time have created massive foreign debts. Egypt's economic strengths include large reserves of natural gas, the Suez Canal, and a huge workforce. But the country is also affected by poverty and high unemployment. Rising numbers of people are overstretching the scarce water supplies and farmland, and causing damage to the environment.

? Did you know?

Egypt is about three times the size of the US state of New Mexico, and four times the size of the UK.

Egypt plays an important role in Middle Eastern as well as African politics. It enjoys close links with other Arab nations while trying to maintain good relations with the West. Egypt's flag, similar to other Arab states such as Syria and Yemen, stresses its closeness with the wider Arab community. Islam, the state religion, influences the country's law, government and everyday life. However, Egypt is not an Islamic state. This causes conflict with some members of its population who want Egypt to become more strictly Islamic. In recent years, Islamic extremists have carried out a string of terrorist attacks in Egypt to try to force change.

Tourism is a major source of foreign earnings in Egypt. Visitors from all over the world come to view the country's ancient ruins and enjoy the scenic beauty of the Nile and Egypt's coasts. Since the 1990s, Egypt's tourist industry has grown rapidly, despite a series of terrorist attacks on tourists and resorts.

PEOPLE AND LANGUAGE

The vast majority of Egyptians can trace their ancestry to the ancient Egyptians and the Arabs, who have lived in Egypt for 1,300 years. Over the centuries, other races such as Greeks, Romans and Turks have added to the ethnic mix. Egypt's population includes a small percentage of Bedouins, an ethnically distinct race who were traditionally nomads. It also includes Berbers, who inhabit certain desert villages, and Nubians, a dark-skinned people of the south. Arabic is the official language, of which there are many regional dialects. French and English are also spoken.

Physical geography

- Land area: 995,450 sq km/384,344 sq miles
- Water area: 6,000 sq km/2,317 sq miles
- Total area: 1,001,450 sq km/386,660 sq miles
- World rank (by area): 30
- Land boundaries: 2,665 km/1,656 miles
- Border countries: Gaza Strip, Israel, Libya, Sudan
- Coastline: 2,450 km/1,522 miles
- Highest point: Mount Catherine (2,629 m/8,625 ft)
- Lowest point: Qattara Depression (-133 m/-436 ft)

Source: CIA World Factbook

◀ Egyptian markets are an exciting blend of smells, sounds, colours and textures. This woman is selling farm produce at a market in Cairo.

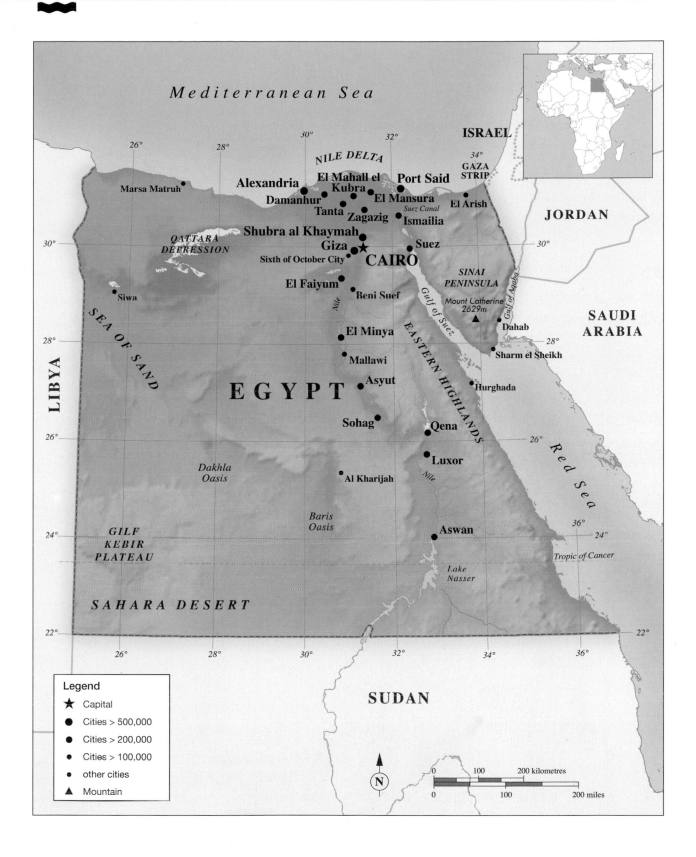

Mediterranean Sea

ISRAEL

NILE DELTA

GAZA STRIP

JORDAN

Marsa Matruh

Alexandria

El Mahall el Kubra

Port Said

Damanhur

El Mansura

El Arish

Tanta

Zagazig

Ismailia

Suez Canal

Shubra al Khaymah

Giza

CAIRO

Suez

Sixth of October City

QATTARA DEPRESSION

El Faiyum

Beni Suef

SINAI PENINSULA

Mount Catherine 2629m

Siwa

El Minya

Dahab

SAUDI ARABIA

EASTERN HIGHLANDS

Sharm el Sheikh

Mallawi

Gulf of Suez

Gulf of Aqaba

SEA OF SAND

Asyut

Hurghada

LIBYA

EGYPT

Sohag

Qena

Red Sea

Dakhla Oasis

Luxor

Al Kharijah

Nile

Baris Oasis

GILF KEBIR PLATEAU

Aswan

Tropic of Cancer

Lake Nasser

SAHARA DESERT

SUDAN

Legend
★ Capital
● Cities > 500,000
● Cities > 200,000
• Cities > 100,000
• other cities
▲ Mountain

N

0   100   200 kilometres

0   100   200 miles

CHAPTER 2

History

Egyptian civilization dates back more than 7,000 years. For more than 3,000 years, Egyptian pharaohs governed the country. From the seventh century BC, Egypt was ruled by a series of foreign powers and only became fully self-governing in the 1950s.

ANCIENT EGYPT

Egyptian civilization began around 5,000 BC with settlements along the Nile. The river's yearly flood spread mineral-rich silt, which allowed farmers to grow sufficient food for everyone. Some people turned from farming to become traders, craft-workers and priests. At first, ancient Egypt consisted of two kingdoms – Upper Egypt in the south, and Lower Egypt in the north. These names relate to the river's upper and lower course. Around 3,200 BC, the two kingdoms were united. The title of pharaoh passed from father to son, so early Egyptian history is divided into dynasties. Three periods of strong dynastic rule were the Old (2,686-2,181 BC), Middle (1,991-1,786 BC) and New (1,554-1,070 BC) kingdoms.

▼ The tombs of Egyptian pharaohs were decorated with paintings depicting the gods and scenes from the ruler's life. Here, the pharaoh Ramses II (1,304-1,237 BC) and his wife Nefertari pay homage to the goddess Hathor.

Science, mathematics, astronomy and the arts flourished in ancient Egypt. In around 3,000 BC, at a time when most other peoples were hunter-gatherers, the Egyptians were farming cereals, making pottery, forging metals, weaving and travelling the Nile by boat. They kept detailed records using a script called hieroglyphics (see page 43), and made complex calculations. Their scientific skills were put to use in the construction of the pyramids as tombs for the pharaohs of the Old Kingdom. These amazing structures represent one of the most incredible feats of engineering ever accomplished.

? Did you know?

Between 1171 and 1250, Egypt was ruled by a Muslim dynasty called the Ayyubids. These were descendants of Saladin (1137-93), a general in the Syrian army who had done battle with the Crusaders, armies of Christian Knights who fought against Muslims for control of Jerusalem in medieval times.

For much of its history, ancient Egypt was protected from invasion by the desert. However, from the seventh century BC, Egypt's wealth and abundant food attracted foreign powers. Around 670 BC, the Assyrians conquered Egypt; they were followed by the Persians, Greeks, and Romans (in 30 BC), and by the Byzantine Empire – the eastern branch of the Roman Empire. During the period of Byzantine rule (c. AD 324-638), most Egyptians became Coptic Christians (see page 49).

Focus on: Mummification

During the Middle Kingdom, a strong belief in the afterlife led to the practice of mummification to preserve human remains. The Egyptians would remove certain organs from the corpse then preserve the body in a special kind of salt for 40 days. They would then treat it with an ointment made from plants and other natural substances, and wrap it in linen strips.

▶ In 2005, near Cairo, Egyptian archaeologists discover a brilliantly coloured casing containing a mummified corpse dating back more than 2,300 years.

MUSLIM RULE

In AD 639, Muslim Arabs moving west across North Africa conquered Egypt, and the country entered a new phase of its history. Under the Arabs, the original people of Egypt converted from Christianity to Islam, and the Arabic script was adopted. Arab dynasties ruled Egypt for most of the following six centuries. The Arabs built the city of Cairo in the ninth century on a site of earlier Egyptian settlement. Under the Fatimids, who ruled Egypt from the tenth century to 1171, Cairo became capital of a large Muslim empire covering most of North Africa and the Middle East. Later, in 1250, a Muslim military caste called the Mamelukes took over. Their power continued even after Egypt's conquest by Ottoman Turks in 1517.

L'ESCADRE DE LA BALTIQUE TRAVERSE LE CANAL DE SUEZ

From around 1800, European powers including France and Britain took an increasing interest in the strategic importance and natural resources of Egypt. In 1798, the French general Napoleon Bonaparte briefly conquered Egypt, but was ousted by Ottoman and British troops in 1801. Muhammad Ali Pasha, an Ottoman officer, became ruler of Egypt. He and his descendants began to modernize the country, improving its infrastructure, farming and education. Under Muhammad's son, Said, a canal was commissioned to cross the narrow isthmus of Suez and link the Mediterranean Sea with the Indian Ocean. The Suez Canal was built by a French company and completed in 1869. It reduced voyages between Europe and the Far East by thousands of kilometres, because ships no longer had to travel round the coast of southern Africa. Both the French and the British were eager to have shares in, and therefore part-control of, this vital link with the East.

BRITISH INFLUENCE

The modernization programmes of Muhammad Ali Pasha and his dynasty left Egypt with heavy debts. To ease the situation, Egypt sold its shares in the Suez Canal to Britain in 1875. In the 1880s, Egypt's government became increasingly disorganized and Britain seized control of the country to protect its interests in the canal.

During the early 1900s, British control over Egypt tightened. During the First World War, Britain made Egypt into a protectorate

◀ In the late 1800s and early 1900s, British and French warships patrolled the Suez Canal as part of a joint venture to maintain European interests in this strategic waterway. A French newspaper from 1904 portrays the scene.

(protected country). The British ran Egypt's administration efficiently and improved agriculture, but they also used the country as a source of raw materials, such as cotton, while hindering industrialization. Anti-British feeling grew. In 1922, Britain granted partial independence to Egypt, but kept its troops there. During the Second World War, Suez was the scene of fighting between Allied and German troops. However, by the end of the war, Britain had largely withdrawn from Egypt, leaving the Ottoman ruler (a descendant of Muhammad Ali Pasha) in control.

In 1945, Egypt became a founding member of the Arab League, an alliance of Arab states. In 1947, the creation of the state of Israel on what had been mostly Arab land in the formerly Ottoman-controlled region of Palestine led to conflict between Israel and the Arab world. Egypt and other Arab nations went to war with Israel, but were defeated. The existence of Israel, and the desire among some Muslims to reject what they believed to be corrupting Western influences, led to growing support for an Islamic party called the Muslim Brotherhood within Egypt. This organization, founded in 1928 by Hassan al-Banna, was active in the 1930s and wanted a strict Islamic government for Egypt.

▲ A British bomber sweeps low over a convoy of French and British troops during manoeuvres in the Egyptian desert during the Second World War.

AN ARAB REPUBLIC

In 1952, a military coup led by a group of officers, including Gamal Abdel Nasser, overthrew Egypt's monarchy and ended 150 years of Ottoman rule. In 1954, Nasser became sole ruler of the new republic. He continued to industrialize and modernize Egypt. At the height of the Cold War, Nasser appealed to the Soviet Union for help to build a dam across the Nile at Aswan, to generate electricity and control the river's annual floods. Nasser suppressed political opposition in Egypt, banning all parties that had existed before 1952 including the Muslim Brotherhood. In 1956, he seized control of the Suez Canal, causing a political crisis (see box opposite) from which he emerged a popular leader.

During the 1960s and 1970s, conflict with Israel continued. In 1967, Israel won a decisive victory over Arab troops in the Six-Day War. Israel occupied the Sinai Peninsula, the neighbouring Gaza Strip and other Arab territory. In 1970, following Nasser's death, a new Egyptian president, Anwar el-Sadat, took office. Sadat changed tack on foreign policy. He broke links with the Soviet Union and courted alliance with the USA to foster economic growth. In 1977-9, Sadat broke with Arab tradition by signing a historic peace treaty, the Camp David Accords, with Israel, in exchange for the Sinai Peninsula. The move was unpopular at home and Egypt was expelled from the Arab League (see

? Did you know?

In 1952 Egypt's ruler, King Faruq, was forced to abdicate in favour of his infant son. The monarchy was abolished altogether the following year.

▼ Soviet leader Nikita Krushchev (waving left) and Egyptian premier Gamal Abdel Nasser (right) greet Egyptian crowds during a visit by Krushchev in 1964. At this time, the alliance between the Soviet Union and Egypt was very strong.

page 11). Unperturbed, Sadat launched an 'open door' policy, seeking alliance and funds from the West to continue modernization.

In 1981, Sadat was assassinated by Islamic extremists. His deputy, Hosni Mubarak, became president and has remained in power ever since. During the 1980s, Mubarak worked hard to restore links with other Arab nations. After Egypt gave support to Iraq during the Iran-Iraq War of 1980-8, it was re-admitted to the Arab League. In 1990-1, Egypt was one of the Arab states to oppose Iraq's seizure of Kuwait and send troops to join the UN force fighting in the Gulf War. Throughout the 1990s, Egypt continued to act as a mediator between the West and the Arab world. In September 2005, Hosni Mubarak was elected to a fifth term as president.

Focus on: The Suez Crisis

In 1956, President Nasser nationalized the Suez Canal, wresting control from France and Britain. In response, and with the aid of France and Britain, Israel attacked Egypt and occupied the Sinai Peninsula. The United Nations (UN) intervened to produce a ceasefire and eventually persuaded the occupiers to withdraw. The canal remained in Egyptian hands, and the former owners were eventually compensated. The crisis made Nasser a hero throughout the Arab world.

▼ In October 1981, soldiers round up suspects following the assassination of Anwar el-Sadat at a military parade in Egypt.

CHAPTER 3

Landscape and Climate

Covering 995,450 sq km (384,344 sq miles), Egypt ranks thirtieth in the world in terms of country area. Its 2,450 km (1,522 miles) of coastline are fringed by extensive coral reefs along the Red Sea.

THE RIVER NILE

The Nile Valley is Egypt's key geographical feature. Some 1,545 km (958 miles) of the river's course lie within Egypt. Each year, spring rain and snowmelt in the mountains of East Africa swell the river level. Before the Aswan Dam was built in the 1960s, the Nile used to burst its banks each year, depositing dark, fertile silt along its valley. Centuries-old cultivation along the Nile has created a green, fertile ribbon up to 15 km (9 miles) wide, with barren desert stretching out to either side.

In the far south at the Sudanese border, the construction of the Aswan Dam on the Nile has created Lake Nasser, one of the world's largest artificial lakes. North of Cairo, the Nile divides into several channels, including the Damietta and Rosetta. Silt deposited by the river here forms a vast triangular delta. This is Egypt's main farming land.

◀ The Suez Canal, seen here as a thin thread of blue, connects the Mediterranean with the western arm of the Red Sea. On the left of the canal lies the Nile Delta, on the right is the barren Sinai Peninsula.

A DESERT LAND

Desert covers 95 per cent of Egypt. There are three main areas: the Western and Eastern Deserts and the Sinai Peninsula. The Western Desert is the largest, covering two-thirds of Egypt. In the north, the Qattara Depression is a deep basin dropping to -133 m (-436 ft) below sea level. Crescent-shaped sand dunes shift across the Sea of Sand in the west, but gravel plains cover most of the desert. The only areas that can be cultivated are around five oases, of which Dakhla is the largest, covering 12,000 hectares. Oases form where water seeping through porous rocks underground reaches a layer of rock through which it cannot pass. The water then runs along the non-porous layer to rise near the surface at oases.

East of the Nile, the Eastern Desert rises gradually from the river valley to the Eastern Highlands, a chain of mountains running parallel to the Red Sea. The Sinai Peninsula consists of a flat coastal plain bordering the Mediterranean, rising to Egypt's highest mountains in the south.

Did you know?

The Nile is the world's longest river, flowing for 6,693 km (4,160 miles). The Egyptian Nile is fed by three main sources: the White Nile, which rises in the mountains of Burundi; the Blue Nile, which rises on the Ethiopian plateau; and the Atbara, which originates in the highlands of Ethiopia.

▼ The jagged mountain chain inland of Na'ama Bay provides a stunning backdrop for the Bedouin settlement of Dahab. The dryness of the climate is evident in the barren terrain.

CLIMATE

Egypt has two main seasons: scorching summers and mild winters. From May to October, summers bring daytime temperatures climbing to 35°C (95°F). However, the fact that the air is dry, not humid, makes the climate more tolerable. From November to April, winter brings more pleasant temperatures, rising to 20°C (68°F) by day and dropping below 10°C (50°F) at night. Desert areas are characterized by even greater extremes of temperature, climbing to 40°C (104°F) daily, but with no clouds to retain the sun's heat falling to near freezing at night.

Winds blowing off the Mediterranean make the north the coolest part of Egypt. The port of Alexandria has summer temperatures of around 29°C (84°F), with winter temperatures of 17°C (62°F). The far south has the hottest climate, with summer temperatures of 41°C (105°F) in Aswan, and winter averages of 23°C (73°F).

Focus on: Winds from the Sahara

The *khamsin* is a hot, dusty wind that regularly blows from the south in March and April and can affect the whole of the country. The wind is named after the Arabic word for 50, which refers to the 50-day period during which the wind may blow for one or two days at a time. The *khamsin* causes temperatures to soar in just a few hours. Huge quantities of red dust carried by the wind wither crops, strip paint from cars, and, because of reduced visibility, even ground aircraft. The gritty dust gets everywhere, including into eyes, mouths and noses. This makes it very difficult to go outside.

▼ In winter, Egypt's sunny skies and warm, dry climate are popular with tourists, especially from northern Europe. This resort at Dahab lies on the Red Sea coast.

Deserts are defined as areas that receive less than 250 mm (10 in) of rain annually. The whole of Egypt falls within this category. Rainfall is highest in the north, where the coastal strip is watered by Mediterranean winter storms. Alexandria is the wettest city, receiving 180 mm (7 in) of rain annually. In the far south, there is little rainfall – for example, Aswan receives an average of just 1 mm (0.04 in) a year. Egypt's low rainfall increases reliance on the Nile. When a rainstorm does occur, water runs rapidly off the dry ground, filling gullies called *wadis* and giving rise to destructive flash floods. In 1994, flash floods in Upper Egypt killed 580 people.

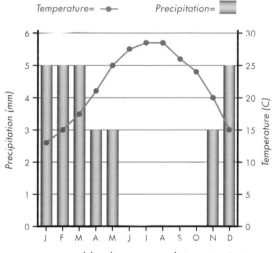

▲ Average monthly climate conditions in Cairo

Focus on: Natural hazards

Egypt's natural hazards include severe drought, flash floods, windstorms, and occasional earthquakes. To the east, the Red Sea marks a boundary between two of the earth's tectonic plates, the African and Arabian plates. As these two plates pull apart, molten lava wells up in the gap to create new sea floor. Newly erupted rock is causing the Red Sea to grow a little wider each year. The plate movements give rise to earthquakes. In 1992, a major earthquake struck Cairo, killing 560 people, injuring 10,000 and destroying thousands of homes.

▼ Palm trees and grasses flourish along a river valley in the mostly dry Sinai Peninsula. These hardy plants are able to withstand long periods of drought when the river level drops.

CHAPTER 4

Population and Settlements

In 2004, Egypt's population was about 77.5 million, making it Africa's most populated country after Nigeria. Egypt's population is extremely unevenly distributed, with an amazing 99 per cent of people living in just 4 per cent of the country's area, along the banks and delta of the Nile and the Suez Canal. The capital, Cairo, is very densely populated, with an estimated 150,000 people in each square kilometre in some districts. In contrast, vast tracts of the desert are virtually uninhabited.

FAST-GROWING POPULATION

Egypt's population is growing rapidly. Since the 1970s, the population has more than doubled, and it is expected to top 90 million by 2020. Even more rapid growth is expected when the third of the population who are currently under the age of 15 start to have children.

Between the years 2000 and 2005, most city families had about three children, but five or more children was common in rural areas. A few decades ago, in the 1970s and 1980s, families with seven children were common. In recent years, the government has tried to slow population growth by promoting birth control, with some success. In 2005, the growth rate was estimated at 1.8 per cent, down from a peak of 3 per cent in 1985. However, many rural families are resistant to the idea of having fewer children. Some strict Muslims believe that birth control is against Islamic law.

CROWDED CITIES

In 2004, 42 per cent of Egypt's population lived in urban areas. The figure looks set to rise to 50 per cent by 2015. Since the 1950s, there has been a strong pattern of rural to urban migration,

◀ Overcrowding and poverty are problems in Egyptian cities, especially in the capital. Slum dwellings like these in Cairo lack adequate sanitation.

especially to Cairo. Most rural dwellers are poor farmers called *fellahin*, who scrape a living raising crops or a few animals on rented land. Jobs are scarce in rural areas, so people move to cities hoping for employment and more money. However, with an estimated 300,000 people moving to urban areas each year, there are not enough jobs to go round. Nor is there enough housing, so many new arrivals end up sleeping on the streets.

Focus on: Alexandria

Alexandria is Egypt's second largest city, with nearly four million people. Founded in 332 BC, it is named after the Greek conqueror Alexander the Great. In ancient times, Alexandria was Europe's foremost centre of learning, with a vast library housing all classical knowledge. (The library burned down in the third century AD.) Alexandria is Egypt's main port and a major industrial centre. It is also the most popular seaside resort among Egyptians, with a milder, wetter climate than Cairo to the south.

▲ Middle-class Egyptians enjoy a comfortable standard of living. This apartment in Cairo is modern, cool and well equipped.

? Did you know?

Between 2000 and 2005, Egypt's population rose by more than one million each year.

Population data

📁 Population: 77.5 million
📁 Population 0-14 yrs: 34%
📁 Population 15-64 yrs: 62%
📁 Population 65+ yrs: 4%
📁 Population growth rate: 2.0%
📁 Population density: 73.3 per sq km/ 189.8 per sq mile
📁 Urban population: 42%
📁 Major cities:
   Alexandria 3,760,000
   Cairo 11,146,000

Source: United Nations and World Bank

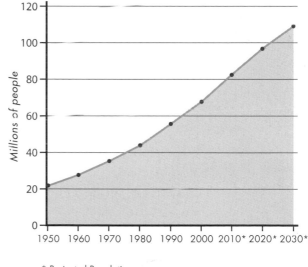

* Projected Population

▲ Population growth, 1950-2030

In the second half of the twentieth century Egypt's cities expanded rapidly. Sprawling suburbs have spread on the outskirts, swallowing up villages and arable land. Even with the rapid expansion, districts such as Cairo's medieval quarter are desperately overcrowded and lacking in essentials such as electricity, clean water and sanitation. The scarcity of housing in Cairo has caused whole families to move into the City of the Dead, a historic cemetery area with stone tombs erected by wealthy families. City authorities have recognized the cemetery as a dwelling place, providing water and electricity. Another large slum has grown up at the site of Cairo's largest rubbish tip. Families here make a living selling scrap metal, plastic and glass.

POLLUTION AND NOISE

Cairo suffers from chronic overcrowding, but it is also plagued by traffic congestion and pollution. The narrow streets of old districts are crammed with buses, cars, donkey carts and pedestrians. A pall of smog hangs in the hot, still air above the city, and many people die each year from breathing problems related to air pollution. The honking of car horns, shouts of street sellers and whirr of air conditioning can be deafening. Following the major building projects that have taken place in the last 30 years, flyovers and high-rise apartments loom over mud-brick slums. When the 1992 earthquake struck (see page 17), flimsy slum dwellings collapsed like stacked cards. However, despite the grime and chaos, Cairo is a dynamic city, a thriving centre for trade and commerce.

▼ Many of Cairo's poorest inhabitants, including new migrants, are forced to find shelter in the city's ancient cemetery, called the 'City of the Dead'.

Since the 1970s, the government has tried to ease overcrowding by constructing new cities in the desert. Over 40 of these new cities are planned by 2020, with the aim of housing up to 50 million people. The new urban areas include Sixth of October City near Cairo, which is linked to the capital by a fast highway. There are no problems with overcrowding and congestion here, but people are reluctant to leave the Nile region for the desert, despite government encouragement. Critics say only the middle classes can afford the housing provided there, and that the new estates are short of facilities such as shops, mosques and community centres, which serve to bring people together.

? Did you know?

Giza was Egypt's third largest city, but it has now merged with Cairo and become part of the greater Cairo area, with over 16 million people.

Focus on: Ethnic make-up

Around 98 per cent of Egypt's population is descended from indigenous Egyptian (Hamitic) and Arab stock. About 1 per cent is Bedouin. Traditionally living as desert wanderers and traders, many Bedouin now live a settled existence either as farmers or city dwellers, often working for the tourist trade. Some 0.8 per cent of Egypt's population are Nubians, a non-Arabic speaking people from near the Sudanese border. The creation of the Aswan Dam and Lake Nasser in the 1960s displaced the Nubian people, who had to move to valley settlements further down the Nile.

▼ Construction is going on in many parts of Egypt to help ease overcrowding in the cities. However, the provision of basic infrastructure, such as roads and sanitation, often lags behind, sometimes for years.

CHAPTER 5

Government and Politics

Egypt has been a republic since the monarchy was abolished in 1953. The 1971 constitution defines Egypt as a socialist democracy, in which everyone over the age of 18 has the right to vote. In practice, democracy in Egypt is limited, with the president possessing vast powers.

SYSTEM OF GOVERNMENT

In the absence of a monarch, Egypt's president wields what is officially described as sovereign power. He is head of state and commander of the armed forces; he also leads the political party that forms the government. The president appoints the cabinet, including the prime minister. In turn, the government appoints local officials, which means the president has power at every level. The Majlis al-Sha'b or People's Assembly is the legislative branch of government. There are 454 members, of which 444 are elected in multi-party elections. Up to another ten members are appointed by the president. Members serve five-year terms. In theory, the People's Assembly is Egypt's law-making body, but in practice it mostly approves policy decisions taken by the president.

▼ Government workers in front of the main government offices in Cairo, known as the Mogamma Building.

In terms of regional government, Egypt is divided into 26 administrative districts, called governorates. The president appoints a governor to head each of these. The governorates are divided into districts and villages, which are administered by various tiers of local government. Egypt has a vast and bureaucratic civil service. The county's legal system is a mixture of Islamic law, English common law and Napoleonic law. The president appoints Egypt's judges; there are no juries. Egypt's armed forces are large in number. Since independence, Egypt's three presidents have all been military men.

? Did you know?

In 2005, Ayman Nour, a leading opposition al-Ghad Party politician, declared that: 'Everyone in Egypt knows that the parliament elections are rigged'. In doing so, he gave voice to a belief held by many ordinary Egyptians.

POWER AND POLITICS

Egypt's ruling party, the National Democratic Party, has been in power since it was formed in 1978. Opposition parties include the New Wafd Party and the Tagammu and al-Ghad parties. The main political opposition comes from the Muslim Brotherhood, an Islamic fundamentalist group that has been officially banned since 1952 (see page 11).

Egypt's president can serve an unlimited number of terms, each lasting six years. Hosni Mubarak, of the National Democratic Party, has held power since 1981, when his predecessor, Anwar el-Sadat, was assassinated. In September 2005, Mubarak was elected to a fifth consecutive term of office. For the first four terms, he was elected by the people in referendums in which he was the only candidate to stand.

◄ Egyptian president, Hosni Mubarak casts his vote in the national elections of 2005. These were hailed as Egypt's first multi-party elections. As widely predicted, President Mubarak won a fifth six-year term, at the age of 77.

In February 2005, the government announced that the September presidential election would be Egypt's first free multi-party election, with other political parties allowed to put forward candidates. In the run-up to the election, opposition parties were allowed to campaign – an activity that would previously have landed them in jail. This is because, since 1981, Egypt has operated under an official state of emergency, which prevents the government's opponents from campaigning publicly. In the 2005 election, the state of emergency was still in place and the opposing parties' activities were still restricted. For example, members of the banned Muslim Brotherhood political movement were not allowed to stand.

Current problems for the government include a rapidly rising population with widespread poverty and overcrowded cities. Unemployment is high, as is inflation. In 2003, the Egyptian pound dropped steeply in value. During the twentieth century, Egypt built up huge international debts through ambitious development projects such as the Aswan Dam, and through war with Israel. In recent years, the government has tried to reduce public debts by cutting government subsidies (financial aid) on food, fuel, transport and other necessities. This has caused considerable hardship for ordinary people and has made the government less popular.

Egypt's government also faces a significant problem with terrorism. Since the 1990s, Islamic fundamentalist groups have carried out a series of attacks on Coptic Christians, industrial targets and, most frequently, tourists (see box opposite). This has harmed the tourist industry, costing the government millions of dollars in lost revenue.

▼ Members of the Muslim Brotherhood attack a bus carrying government supporters during the 2005 election. In November 2005, police arrested 200 Muslim Brotherhood activists.

Focus on: Islamic fundamentalism

Islamic fundamentalists are Muslims who want strict Islamic law, called *Sharia* law, to be applied in Egypt. They want Egypt to become an Islamic state, instead of one proclaiming freedom of religious practice. They also want Islam to be the state religion. There are a number of Islamic groups, including the Muslim Brotherhood and Islamic Jihad. The latter group carried out the assassination of President Sadat in 1981. (President Sadat was unpopular with many Arab extremists: he had made peace with Israel in 1977 and had been rewarded for this with aid from the USA.)

During his first two terms of office, President Mubarak allowed the Muslim Brotherhood to be more openly active, but he has since clamped down on their activities. Some experts believe that this has made the party more popular. The Muslim Brotherhood claims that Egypt will not be a true democracy until their party is unbanned, but to date the government ban remains in place. Since the 1990s, another group, Al-Gama'a al-Islamiya, has carried out a string of shootings and bombings, including the massacre of 58 tourists and four Egyptians in Luxor in 1997. Tourists were the target of further attacks in the cities of Taba and Nuweiba in 2004. In July 2005, bombs at the Red Sea resort of Sharm el Sheikh killed 63 people. The Egyptian government has tried to stamp out terrorism, but its attempts have led to accusations of torture and human rights abuses by the campaign group Amnesty International.

▼ Egyptian security forces struggle to maintain order as votes are counted in the final stage of the parliamentary elections in 2005.

CHAPTER 6

Energy and Resources

Egypt's natural resources include minerals and fossil fuels, farmland, fish and fresh water. However, these resources are relatively scarce, and are being overstretched by the growing population.

ENERGY SOURCES AND USE

Petroleum and natural gas are among Egypt's most precious resources. Known oil reserves are located in the Eastern and Western Deserts, the Sinai Peninsula, and offshore in the Gulf of Suez and Red Sea. Oil production rose in the 1980s, but Egypt's oil industry was hit by the changing price of oil on the world market in the 1990s. The price of oil rose and fell internationally in response to world demand for oil, and stocks of the fuel available internationally. Oil production in Egypt has fallen since 1995. Egypt's gas is even more important than oil. Natural gas has been located along the Mediterranean coast around Alexandria, and in the delta and Western Desert. Offshore gas fields are becoming increasingly productive, and those located in deeper waters will provide energy and income in future.

Hydro-electricity (HEP) is an important energy source. In the late 1990s, HEP provided 25 per cent of Egypt's electricity. This percentage has since fallen as natural gas is used more. In 2002, HEP provided 16.3 per cent of Egypt's electricity, with natural gas supplying almost 76 per cent, and oil 7.5 per cent. Apart from HEP, renewable forms of energy make no significant contribution, despite the potential for solar, wind and even wave power.

? *Did you know?*

Oil was discovered in Egypt as far back as 1896. The first known oil fields were located in the Gulf of Suez.

▼ Oil storage tankers stand at a refinery on the Egyptian coast.

Energy data

- Energy consumption as % of world total: 0.5%
- Energy consumption by sector (% of total),
  Industry: 44
  Transportation: 21.7
  Agriculture: 0.7
  Services: 2.8
  Residential: 24
  Other: 6.8
- CO_2 emissions as % of world total: 0.5
- CO_2 emissions per capita in tonnes p.a.: 1.65

Source: World Resources Institute

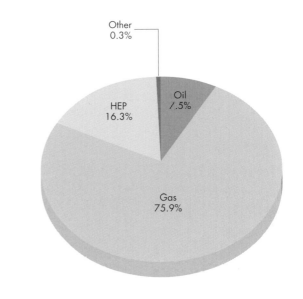

Other 0.3%

Oil 7.5%

HEP 16.3%

Gas 75.9%

▲ Electricity production by type

Focus on: The Aswan Dam

The Aswan Dam was constructed between 1960 and 1968 with the help of Soviet funds and engineers. This massive engineering project, which created Lake Nasser, involved relocating the ancient temple of Abu Simbel, which stood on the banks of the Nile. Every stone of the gigantic monument had to be painstakingly removed and reassembled on a higher site, which was landscaped to match the original. Nubian settlements also had to be relocated. Since it opened, the Aswan Dam has provided cheap electricity and prevented droughts and destructive floods. However, it has greatly altered the Nile environment (see pages 28 and 29).

◀ The construction of the Aswan Dam allowed 910,000 hectares of desert land to be converted to farmland. The dam began operating in 1968.

▲ A donkey-operated water wheel raises water from the Nile to irrigate fields by the river. Simple devices like this have been in use since ancient times.

During the early 2000s, natural gas was used to supply homes, factories and vehicle fuel. The government has encouraged conversion to gas because it is not only cheaper but also cleaner (see page 54). Natural gas and oil are leading exports, but an expanding domestic market diminishes the profits to be gained by exporting oil. Egypt lacks sufficient finance to develop newly discovered oil and gas fields and to refine fuels. In recent years, it has had to import refined oil while exporting crude, because it lacks refineries.

MINERALS

Apart from fossil fuels, Egypt's minerals are not abundant. Minerals extracted include iron ore, manganese, phosphate, gypsum, dolomite, zinc and lead. The mountains of the Eastern Desert are the richest mining area, yielding lead, iron,

zinc and salt. Clay, limestone, marble and granite are mined for construction. Limestone is used in the manufacture of cement, a major industry.

FISHING AND FARMING

Fish are harvested from coastal waters and inland wetlands. The Nile Delta lakes, the Red Sea and Lake Qarun near Cairo are the most productive fisheries. The building of the Aswan Dam has caused fish stocks to decline in the delta and in coastal waters to the north. Tomb paintings from ancient Egypt and historical records dating from the 1700s and 1800s show that the Nile and its delta were once fine hunting grounds, but overfishing and overhunting have wiped out or reduced stocks of birds, mammals and fish. Of 47 species of fish caught in the Nile Delta in the early twentieth century, 30 are now extinct and many of the surviving 17 are scarce.

Arable land covers just 2.7 per cent of Egypt. Most of this land lies in the delta and along the banks of the Nile, which supplies almost all of Egypt's fresh water. However, date palm plantations also surround desert oases where groundwater reserves can be tapped.

Agriculture is almost entirely dependent on irrigation. For thousands of years, farmers relied on the Nile's yearly flood to water crops. They dug shallow basins in fields alongside the Nile, and these filled with floodwater. Crops planted when the floods subsided were nourished by river silt. From the 1800s onwards, the construction of dams, reservoirs and canals provided more reliable irrigation. In the 1970s, the Aswan Dam transformed agriculture, providing year round irrigation. However, with floodwaters no longer providing rich silt, farmers had to buy chemical fertilizers instead.

Crops grown in Egypt include cotton, rice, beans, sugar cane, tomatoes and dates. Goats and sheep are reared for meat, wool and milk, while cattle and water buffalo are used mainly as draught animals. Both small- and large-scale farming are practised in Egypt. Large commercial farms grow cash crops such as sugar cane and cotton using modern methods. At the other end of the scale, peasant farmers (*fellahin*) grow crops mostly for their own needs using primitive ploughs and sickles. Under Islamic law, land is divided among a farmer's children, so the plots of *fellahin* become smaller with each generation.

▼ On the banks of the Nile river, a *fellah* clears a temporary dam to channel precious water on to a lower terrace, where crops are being grown.

CHAPTER 7

Economy and Income

Egypt is classed as a less economically developed country. This means it is one of the world's less wealthy countries, and its industries are not as efficient as those of so-called developed countries. Economic growth is hampered by several factors, including scarce natural resources and inefficient working practices. In 2003, Egypt's economy grew by 1.4 per cent.

During the 1950s and 1960s, Egypt industrialized fairly rapidly, having freed itself from British control which had held back industrialization. Reforms made in the 1960s encouraged economic growth. In 1965, the average yearly earnings per person in Egypt amounted to just US$180. By 2004, this figure (called the Gross National Income, or GNI per capita) had risen to US$1,310. This average income is higher than in many developing economies, including China, but much lower than in developed countries such as the USA, France and Japan.

In the period following independence, Egypt nationalized many large- and medium-scale industries, including those of cotton and steel. In the longer term, this has led to inefficient working practices, with too many staff and outdated methods and equipment. The cotton and steel industries are still largely state-owned, but many other businesses have now been sold to private owners. This has increased efficiency and profits. In 2004, the government made a series of economic reforms, revising taxation and cutting subsidies – measures aimed at improving Egypt's competitiveness in the world.

SERVICES, AGRICULTURE AND INDUSTRY

Service industries are the largest sector of the economy. They include jobs in government, trade, transport, communication, tourism, banking and education. Government, banking and trade are major employers. Tourism and the film and music industries (see pages 50-53)

◀ Bags of cement await transport from a cement works near Cairo. As cement is widely used in government backed building schemes, its manufacture is big business in Egypt.

make important contributions to the economy. In the years following independence, Egypt guaranteed jobs in the civil service for all university graduates. These jobs were secure but poorly paid, and many government workers were forced to take a second job, such as taxi driving. In recent years, the government has reduced the number of government workers. In 2001, 51 per cent of the workforce was employed in service industries, which all together yielded around half of the country's national income.

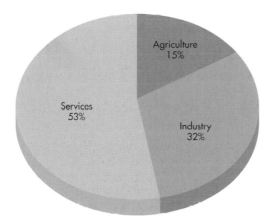

▲ Contribution by sector to national income

Agriculture 15%
Services 53%
Industry 32%

Economic data

- Gross National Income (GNI) in US$: 90,129,000,000
- World rank by GNI: 44
- GNI per capita in US$: 1,310
- World rank by GNI per capita: 131
- Economic growth: 1.4%

Source: World Bank

Did you know?

In 1996, the vehicle manufacturer Mercedes set up a car assembly plant in one of the new desert cities, Sixth of October (see page 21). These cities are among the major building projects launched by the government since 1979.

▶ Dates are picked by hand on a plantation in Saqqara village, near Cairo. The worker places the fruit in a suspended basket to avoid damaging it.

Over the last 50 years, the percentage of Egyptians working in agriculture has fallen steeply, from 57 per cent in 1960 to 33 per cent in 2001. In 2003, this sector provided just 15 per cent of the GDP. The most important farm products are cotton, rice, maize, wheat, beans, sugar cane, oranges, potatoes, tomatoes, and also livestock such as sheep and goats. Until the 1970s, Egypt grew enough food to meet its own needs, but it has since had to import food to sustain its growing population.

In 2001, industry employed 16 per cent of the workforce for around a third of the GDP. Cotton and textiles are the most important products in Egypt, followed by processed foods, chemicals, fertilizers, pharmaceuticals, iron and steel. Cairo and Alexandria are the main centres of manufacturing. In recent years, the government has used measures such as tax cuts to encourage industries to relocate to new cities. Information technology and electronics equipment are expanding sectors in newly developed locations such as Pyramids Technology Valley near Cairo.

WORKING CONDITIONS

In 2004, Egypt's workforce was estimated at 20.7 million. In a sense this huge workforce is one of Egypt's greatest assets. However, unemployment is a major problem. In 2004, 10.9 per cent of workers were unemployed, with young people aged 15-30 finding it particularly difficult to get a job. Unemployment looks set to rise as the high proportion of the population currently under the age of 15 leaves school and searches for a job.

Outside the officially registered workforce, a great many Egyptians work in the informal sector, for example, selling goods on the street, cleaning shoes or cars, repairing machinery or working in certain industries that do not pay tax. This thriving sector makes a major contribution to the economy, but the government is trying to persuade more of these mainly small businesses to register in order to increase tax revenues.

▼ A coppersmith makes a tea tray in the Khan al-Khalili bazaar in Cairo's Islamic quarter.

In the 1950s, very few women worked outside the home. The proportion of women in the workforce has risen slowly but steadily since the 1960s, from 25 per cent in 1965, to 30 per cent in 2000. Most women work in service industries, including in government jobs. There are relatively few women working in industry. In the private sector, women are often paid less than men for the same work. Islamic law forbids women from working in the military, police and in religious institutions, but a growing number of Egyptian women are working as professionals, for example, as doctors, dentists and teachers.

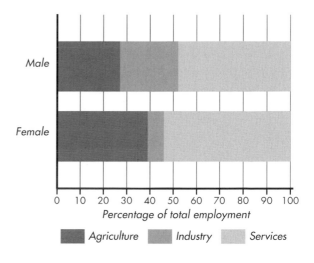

▲ Labour force by sector and gender

Focus on: The cotton industry

Cotton is Egypt's most valuable cash crop. The country leads the world in the production of long-fibred cotton, which is used to make tough, durable fabrics. Egypt's cotton industry grew rapidly during the American Civil War (1861-5) when Union forces fought Confederates over the issue of slavery. Union forces laid siege to ports in the southern USA to prevent the south from exporting cotton, its most lucrative crop.

Cotton producing nations such as Egypt took advantage of the blockage of the southern ports to become major cotton exporters. In 2004, about a quarter of all Egyptian workers engaged in manufacturing worked in the cotton industry, mostly in state-owned factories. However, these factories often do not run very efficiently because they have old-fashioned equipment.

◄ Hawkers push a barrowload of bread for sale on the El-Giza bridge in Cairo. Street traders form a significant part of Egypt's thriving informal economy.

CHAPTER 8

Global Connections

◀ Rachid Mohamed Rachid, the Egyptian minister for Foreign Trade and Industry (far right) links arms with delegates from other nations at the World Trade Summit in 2005. The delegates are demonstrating their support for moves towards fair trade, which should benefit less well-off nations, such as Egypt.

In 1945, as the Second World War ended, Egypt made two alliances that were to affect its future profoundly. It became a founder member of the United Nations and of the Arab League. Maintaining good international relations has been a top priority in Egypt ever since.

TRADE PARTNERS

Since the days of ancient Egypt, foreign trade has been vital to the country's economy. In the early 2000s, Egypt's chief exports were gas, oil, cotton fibres and textiles, metals, chemicals and fruit. In 2004, these goods went to Italy (13.1 per cent), the USA (11.6 per cent), the UK (7.5 per cent) and Germany (5.1 per cent), followed by Spain and France. In the same year, Egypt's chief imports were machinery, vehicles, food, chemicals, wood and fuel, which came from the

USA (13.2 per cent), Germany (7.2 per cent), Italy (7.1 per cent), France (6.1 per cent), followed by China, the UK and Saudi Arabia. For many years, Egypt has spent more on importing goods than it has earned for its own exports. In 2005, for example, Egypt imported goods worth US$24.1 billion, but exported only US$14.3 billions' worth. This means that Egypt had a considerable trade deficit (shortfall) of around US$9.8 billion in 2005.

Egypt relies on 'invisible earnings' to reduce its trade gap. These include fees from the Suez Canal and earnings sent back by Egyptians working abroad. Skilled Egyptian graduates, such as engineers, are in demand abroad. In 2004, an estimated five million Egyptians were working elsewhere, mostly in oil-rich states such as Saudi Arabia and the United

Arab Emirates, and also in Europe. The USA also has a significant number of Egyptian immigrants. Meanwhile, an estimated five million Sudanese were working in Egypt.

EGYPT AND THE ARAB WORLD

Egypt maintains close links with other Arab nations both in Africa and the Middle East. In 1958, it formed the Union of Arab States with Syria and Yemen, but this loose union broke up in 1961. In 1979, as a result of the Camp David Peace Accords with Israel, Egypt was isolated from the rest of the Arab world and expelled from the Arab League. However, Egypt had restored these links by 1990. Relations with neighbouring Libya deteriorated in the 1970s, but have since become close.

? Did you know?

From 1979 to 2004, Egypt received an average of US$2.2 billion aid yearly from the USA.

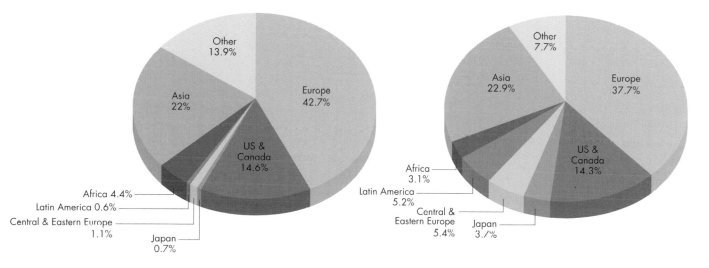

▲ Destination of exports by major trading region

Europe 42.7%
US & Canada 14.6%
Asia 22%
Other 13.9%
Africa 4.4%
Latin America 0.6%
Central & Eastern Europe 1.1%
Japan 0.7%

▲ Origin of imports by major trading region

Europe 37.7%
US & Canada 14.3%
Asia 22.9%
Other 7.7%
Africa 3.1%
Latin America 5.2%
Central & Eastern Europe 5.4%
Japan 3.7%

► Seated left to right are Anwar el-Sadat; the US president, Jimmy Carter; and the Israeli premier, Menachem Begin. This photo was taken in September 1978 at the signing of two agreements at the White House, Washington DC, USA. The agreements are known as the Camp David Peace Accords.

▲ Egyptian president Hosni Mubarak was one of many leaders who attended the 2005 Arab League summit meeting in Algeria.

Egypt also maintains a reasonably successful working relationship with Sudan to the south, despite an ongoing territory dispute over the Hala'ib triangle along the Red Sea coast. This area lies north of the Egypt-Sudan border, which was set at latitude 22° north in 1899. Maintaining good relations with Sudan and other East African nations, such as Uganda and Ethiopia, is vital for Egypt since the Nile flows through these countries before reaching Egypt.

Egypt is widely seen as a cultural leader among Arab nations in terms of Islamic learning, media and the arts, including film and music (see pages 41 and 47). Cairo's oldest mosque, Al-Azhar, is one of the highest authorities within Islam.

The headquarters of the Arab League is now in Cairo, and many secretary generals of the league have been Egyptian. For many years Egypt has acted as a mediator both among Arab nations and between the Arab world and the West and Israel, including during peace negotiations in the Middle East (see box opposite).

INTERNATIONAL RELATIONS

Egypt is known internationally for its history and culture. Tourists from all over the world come to view its ancient tombs and temples. In recent decades, Egypt has worked hard to forge good international relations, especially with powerful, wealthy nations such as the USA, the UK and other European countries. Since independence, Egyptian presidents have cultivated close links, first with the Soviet Union and later with the USA, with the aim of securing funds for projects such as the Aswan

Dam. The 1978 Peace Accords with Israel ushered in an era of 'open door' or increased trade with the West. In 1990-1, Egypt's opposition to Iraq's invasion of Kuwait was important economically, as it led to the cancellation of US$7 billion in foreign debt. For several decades, Egypt has been the second largest receiver of US aid after Israel. Economic reforms made in recent years have largely been to meet conditions set by loaning agencies such as the World Bank (see page 30).

? Did you know?

In 1991, the number of troops sent by Egypt to join UN forces fighting against Iraq was second only to the number of US troops fighting there.

▼ US service personnel aboard the aircraft carrier USS *Washington* in the Suez Canal. The USA is one of the Western nations to maintain a regular military presence in the canal.

Focus on: Egypt and Israel

The Middle East has been an area of political instability since the end of the Second World War, when Israel was created from part of the region of Palestine. Egypt was the first Arab nation to make peace with Israel, following a series of wars between the two countries in 1948, 1956, 1967 and 1973. This move cemented Egypt's friendship with the USA. The 1978 Camp David Accords helped to establish Egypt as a negotiator in the troubled region. Egypt has since helped in negotiations between Israel and other Arab states. In 2004, Egypt assisted with peace talks between Israel and the Palestinians. In the same year, some 70,000 Palestinians fled Gaza to seek refuge in Egypt, but they have not yet been offered asylum. Israel withdrew from the Gaza Strip in 2005.

CHAPTER 9

Transport and Communications

Egypt's infrastructure is reasonably modern. The Suez Canal is one of the world's most important transport links, bringing in US$2 billion in revenue annually from 2000 to 2005.

ROAD AND RAIL

Egypt has 64,000 km (39,769 miles) of roads, of which some 50,000 km (over 31,000 miles) are paved. The main highways run along the Nile Valley and northern coast, linking cities such as Aswan, Luxor, Cairo, El Faiyum, Alexandria and Port Said. Remote oases are linked by desert roads that make for monotonous driving and dangerous conditions when sandstorms blow.

City streets are crowded with cars, trucks, taxis, buses, scooters, donkey carts, bicycles and pedestrians. Roads are congested and very noisy during rush hours, with motorists routinely

Transport & communications data

- ▷ Total roads: 64,000 km/39,769 miles
- ▷ Total paved roads: 49,984 km/31,060 miles
- ▷ Total unpaved roads: 14,016 km/8,709 miles
- ▷ Total railways: 5,063 km/3,146 miles
- ▷ Airports: 87
- ▷ Cars per 1,000 people: 22.8
- ▷ Mobile phones per 1,000 people: 84.5
- ▷ Personal computers per 1,000 people: 21.9
- ▷ Internet users per 1,000 people: 39.3

Source: World Bank and CIA World Factbook

▼ Donkey carts are among the many modes of transport that share the streets of Egypt's cities.

sounding their horns. Traffic fumes cause considerable pollution, although this has been reduced by the conversion of many vehicles to natural gas. Car ownership is far less common in Egypt than in developed countries such as the USA, so many people travel between cities using buses, which range from modern air-conditioned coaches to rattling boneshakers.

In the early 2000s, Egypt's rail network consisted of 5,063 km (3,146 miles) of track. The network is quite old – one-third of the

track was laid before 1870 – and in need of some modernization. Rail travel is inexpensive because of government subsidies. Like the main highways, the rail network follows the Nile Valley and northern coast, running from Aswan

? Did you know?

Cairo taxi drivers are fast and sometimes reckless – leading to large numbers of serious accidents. For this reason, the vehicles are nicknamed 'flying coffins'.

Focus on: The Suez Canal

The Suez Canal is the world's third longest artificial waterway, covering a distance of 167 km (103 miles). Running between Port Said on the Mediterranean and Suez on the Red Sea, it utilizes a series of natural lakes. When completed in 1869, it was about 1 km (0.6 miles) wide, and ships used the lakes as passing places. The canal has since been deepened and widened several times. Between 2000 and 2005, 6 per cent of the world's shipping passed though Suez, but this

volume could be even greater if the canal were deep enough to take the largest oil tankers when fully laden. There are plans to deepen the canal to 30m (98 ft) within the next ten years, which would allow almost all supertankers to pass through. Laden supertankers travelling from the Gulf States to Europe currently have to go by way of southern Africa, or use the SUMED (Suez-Mediterranean) pipeline to transport their oil from the Red Sea to the northern coast.

◀ Passengers ride the metro in Cairo, in an area where the line runs above ground.

▲ The tall sails of *feluccas* have been seen on the Nile since the time of the pharaohs. These elegant craft are still used to carry cargo and passengers, including tourists.

to Alexandria. Cairo has a busy metro (light railway with much underground track) with two lines, one running east of the river and the other from the centre to Giza. It is fast, clean and efficient. All trains have a carriage reserved for women, in accordance with Islamic tradition.

WATER AND AIR TRAVEL

The ancient Egyptians were among the first people to build boats and sail on exploratory voyages. In early times, the Nile was Egypt's main highway, used to transport crops, passengers and the huge stones required to build the pyramids. Later, in medieval times, some Arab peoples were expert sailors with navigation skills superior to those of European mariners. The Nile still functions as a highway,

as it did in ancient times. Egyptian craft called *feluccas* with triangular sails have plied the Nile for centuries, and can still be seen there today, along with catamarans, cruisers and barges.

Egypt now has 3,500 km (2,170 miles) of navigable waterways, including the Alexandria-Cairo waterway, Lake Nasser and the Suez Canal. Main ports include Alexandria, Port Said, Suez and Aswan. Ferries transport passengers across the Red Sea and the Nile.

In 2004, Egypt had 87 airports, of which 70 had paved runways. Cairo, Luxor, Alexandria, Hurghada, Aswan and Nuweiba are the busiest

? Did you know?

The ancient Egyptians dug an irrigation canal across the Suez isthmus. At high tide, boats could pass between the Mediterranean Sea and Red Sea. This first Suez Canal later silted up.

airports. Cairo, Alexandria, Luxor, Aswan, Sharm el Sheikh and Hurghada deal with international traffic. The national carrier, EgyptAir, runs services between major cities and also operates international flights.

MEDIA AND COMMUNICATIONS

Egypt's communications were updated in the 1990s and are fairly modern. Internet access and mobile phone coverage are available in urban areas. In 2003, only about 1 in 50 people owned a personal computer, but about 1 in 25 used the Internet. Mobile phone use has risen rapidly since 1997, when just one person in every 1,000 had a mobile, to about 1 in 12 in 2003.

Egyptian media, especially film and television, are a major influence in the Arab world. The state broadcasting company, Egypt Radio Television Union (ERTU), dominates broadcasting, with two national, six regional and numerous satellite TV channels, and eight national radio networks in 2005. In 2003, the state monopoly of TV and radio was broken by the launch of the private TV networks, Dream TV and Al-Mihwar TV, and by commercial radio stations. Egypt's booming film industry supplies films and TV programmes

to many Arab nations, with Media Production City, the industry's base, striving to become the 'Hollywood of the East'.

Egyptian newspapers are among the most widely read in the Arab world. They include the state-owned *Al-Ahram* and *Al-Akhbar*. Opposition parties have their own newspapers, including *Al-Wafd* and *Al-Ahali*. Although often critical of the government, these are careful not to go too far as, under the state of emergency, those who 'insult' the government can be jailed. *The Middle East Times* and *Al-Ahram Weekly* are both English-language weeklies.

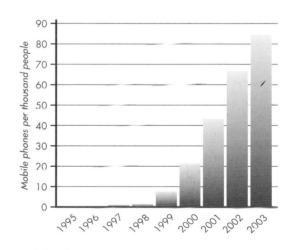

▲ Mobile phone use, 1995-2003

◀ Children from a poor district of Cairo are taught how to use computers and access the Internet.

CHAPTER 10

Education and Health

Since the 1990s, education and health have become high priorities for the Egyptian government. Poverty and the country's rapidly growing population are the main obstacles to improvements in both fields.

EDUCATION

In 2003, an estimated 57 per cent of Egyptian adults could read and write. This figure is low compared with levels in Western countries such as the USA and UK, where some 99 per cent of people are literate. However, Egyptian literacy levels improved greatly during the twentieth century. In the 1940s, only around 20 per cent of the population could read and write. This had risen to 31 per cent by 1970 and to 43 per cent by 1985. Literacy is lower among women than men, with just 47 per cent of women able to read and write in 2003. However, this figure has risen quite rapidly, as only 10 per cent of women were literate around 30 years ago.

In Egypt, schooling is supposed to be compulsory between the ages of six and 15, but is only enforced for children up to the age of 12. Between 1995 and 2003, 85 per cent of children attended primary school but only 50 per cent went on to secondary school. The remaining children, mainly from poor backgrounds, leave school to help out at home or earn money for their families. Most children attend state schools where schooling is provided free, but a small percentage of middle-class children go to private, fee-paying schools. Secondary schooling can be general or technical, to prepare for a particular career. Around 10 per cent of Egyptian children continue beyond secondary school to some form of higher education.

◀ Morning assembly at a middle-class school in a Cairo suburb involves saying prayers and singing the national anthem.

In the 1960s and 1970s, Egypt's education system was seriously under-funded, resulting in a shortage of schools especially in rural areas. City schools were also under-resourced, with large classes. For many pupils, the school day was short to allow several shifts of children to be taught each day. Teachers were poorly paid and many gave private lessons to earn extra money. Since the 1990s, the government has invested heavily in education. Between 1996 and 2001, thousands of new schools opened, and this resulted in smaller classes and improved resources.

◀ Female students at an Islamic school in Cairo sit a mid-year examination.

Education and health

- Life expectancy at birth male: 67.6
- Life expectancy at birth female: 70.8
- Infant mortality rate per 1,000: 33
- Under five mortality rate per 1,000: 39
- Physicians per 1,000 people: 2.1
- Health expenditure as % of GDP: 4.9%
- Education expenditure as % of GDP: n/a
- Primary net enrolment: 85%
- Pupil-teacher ratio, primary: 22.2
- Adult literacy as % age 15+: 57

Source: United Nations Agencies and World Bank

Focus on: Ancient Egyptian script

The ancient Egyptians developed a form of writing called hieroglyphics consisting of picture symbols, some of which have a phonetic value. Writers or scribes wrote mainly on papyrus – paper made from reeds – and on clay tablets and stone monuments. For many centuries, no one could read hieroglyphics. Then, in 1822, a French scholar, Jean François Champollion, decoded the script with the help of the Rosetta stone, an inscription in both Egyptian and Greek characters. This allowed historians to learn much more about Egypt's ancient past.

In accordance with Islamic tradition, most schools are single sex, although some schools, especially private ones, are trying mixed classes. Pupils are under great pressure to pass end-of-year examinations.

Egypt's higher education institutions are highly regarded in the Arab world. There are 13 public universities, of which the largest is Cairo. There are also private universities. Egyptian graduates are highly trained, and qualified engineers and teachers find it easy to obtain employment in other Arab countries. Under President Sadat, all college graduates were guaranteed government jobs, but this is no longer the case.

▼ The central courtyard of the Al-Azhar mosque in Cairo is flanked by the theological college, which dates from the fourteenth century. Al-Azhar means 'the most blooming'.

? Did you know?

Al-Azhar University in Cairo was founded in 970. It is one of the world's most important centres for Arab teaching. Women students have only been admitted since 1962.

HEALTH

In recent decades, life expectancy has risen rapidly following improvements in public health and sanitation. In the 1960s, the average life expectancy was 46 years; this rose to 62 years by 1990, and 69 years in 2003. Improved healthcare has reduced the number of deaths among infants and the under-fives, which has caused the overall population figure to rise. Realizing that a rapidly growing population would cause greater poverty and a strain on natural resources, the government launched a major birth control drive in the 1980s. This has

proved successful particularly in urban areas, bringing the population growth rate down to around 2 per cent by 2005. Birth rates are still higher in rural areas.

Typhoid, cholera and hepatitis are diseases caused by contact with polluted water. These bacterial infections are common in poorer parts of Egypt where people lack access to clean water. Bilharzia, a tiny parasitic worm that lurks by rivers and lakes, causes kidney and digestive disorders. Some other health problems relatively common in Egypt, such as diabetes and high blood pressure, may be partly caused by an unhealthy lifestyle, including smoking, a fatty diet, and not taking enough exercise. In 2001, less than 0.1 per cent of Egypt's population was estimated to have HIV/AIDS.

In 2002, the Egyptian government spent 4.9 per cent of the GDP on healthcare. Recent decades have seen some improvements in public heathcare, but hospitals and clinics are still overstretched in large cities, and scarce in rural areas. In 2000, Egypt had an average of 2.1 doctors for every 1,000 patients. While low, this represents about double the figure in the 1980s.

National healthcare is free or inexpensive, but basic, and those who can afford to do so go to private clinics or even abroad for medical care. Better pay and conditions in private medicine tempt staff away from the public sector.

? Did you know?

In Egypt, 40 per cent of hospital admissions are the result of bacterial infections or intestinal parasites.

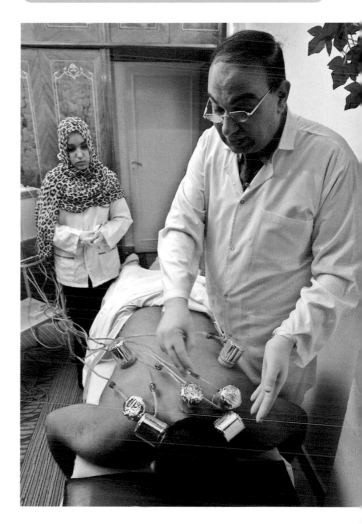

▲ Alternative medicine as practised in Egypt. A practitioner of 'cupping' applies glass jars to a patient's body. Air is sucked from the jars to stimulate the patient's tissue and blood flow.

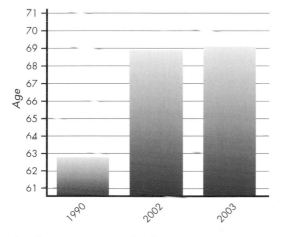

▲ Life expectancy at birth, 1990-2003

CHAPTER 11

Culture and Religion

Egypt's rich cultural heritage, which began at the time of the pharaohs, has been passed down through the years. Religious beliefs and practices date back to the coming of Islam in the seventh century AD and beyond, to ancient and early Christian times.

THE ARTS

Egypt's artistic tradition dates from around 3,000 BC, when the artists of ancient Egypt excelled at sculpture, painting and jewellery- and furniture-making. The magnificent tombs of the pharaohs were decorated with carvings and paintings showing scenes from daily life in ancient Egypt. From the seventh century AD, Islamic architects built fine mosques decorated with intricate carvings. One of the most famous

artistic movements of more recent times that was popular in Egypt was modernism. In the early twentieth century, visual artists, such as sculptor Mahmoud Mukhtar (1891-1934), blended Eastern and Western influences in their work.

Egypt's literary tradition is also long established. From around 300 BC-AD 300, Alexandria was a renowned centre for Arab and Greek learning. There is also a rich tradition of oral storytelling that is centuries

▼ The pyramids at Giza were built to bury three pharaohs of the Old Kingdom during the golden age of ancient Egyptian culture. They were considered one of the Seven Wonders of the World in ancient times.

old. In the mid-twentieth century, writers Tawfiq al-Hakim and Taha Hussein were acclaimed for their portrayal of Egyptian society. In 1988, Naguib Mahfouz became the first writer in Arabic to win the Nobel Prize for literature. More recently, novelists such as Sonallah Ibrahim and Nawal El Saadawi have used the form of allegory to voice criticism of the government. By adopting this literary form they have been able to deliver their message and avoid falling foul of strict censorship laws.

Many forms of music are heard in Egypt, with regional styles using different instruments. For example, *saiyidi* music of southern Egypt is played on the two-sided drum and wooden trumpet, while delta peasant music, or *felahi*, is performed on the two-string viol and oboe-like *mismar*. Egypt's best-loved singer, Umm Kalthoum, sang popular love songs; millions mourned when she died in 1975. Since the 1970s, new musical forms have evolved. *Shaabi* or 'people music' has a fast beat with words drawing on modern life and culture. Al-Jeel, or 'the generation', combines Nubian and Bedouin rhythms with a synthesized disco beat.

RELIGION AND SOCIAL CUSTOMS

Today some 89 per cent of Egyptians follow the Islamic religion, of which nearly all are Sunni Muslims. Islam plays a major role in daily life. As in other Muslim countries, the call to prayer is heard five times daily. City dwellers, rural farmers and desert nomads stop what they are doing and kneel to face the holy city of Mecca, in Saudi Arabia, to say their prayers. Islamic *Sharia* law influences Egyptian customs. For example, the government collects donations from the wealthy and distributes them to the poor in obedience to the Islamic code of almsgiving.

▼ A Sufi dancer is accompanied by musicians who create a hypnotic rhythm for the dancer to move to. Sufism is a semi-mystical branch of the religion of Islam, and dancing is part of its expression.

Over the centuries, Egypt has developed a form of Islam that is somewhat different from Muslim culture elsewhere. For example, saints are more prominent in Egypt than in most Muslim countries – a tradition that is probably influenced by the ancient Egyptian custom of reverence for the dead. Every town and village has its own Muslim saint, who is revered by the local people in a practice suggestive of ancient times, when each community had its own protective god (see box opposite).

Islam touches every aspect of life. In Muslim culture, men and women have roles that are more separate than they are in the West. In Islam, the man predominates as head of the household. He goes out to earn money while the woman traditionally stays at home to care for the children. In modern Egypt these traditional roles are less obvious and it is common to see women in employment or engaged in activities beyond the home. But males and females are still schooled separately in the main, and segregated during worship and in some public places, such as on trains. Islamic fundamentalists feel that Egyptian culture has been corrupted by anti-Islamic influences. Some of them form groups, such as the Muslim Brotherhood, and call for a return to strict Islamic law.

Islamic tradition also influences how people dress. The traditional dress for men is the *galabiyah*, an ankle-length cotton garment. Islamic custom dictates that women wear a veil and long, flowing robes that cover the body in public. Among city dwellers, Western dress is more commonly worn by men and women,

▲ A *muezzin* gives the call to prayer from a Cairo mosque. Today, the calls broadcast from many mosques are amplified electronically.

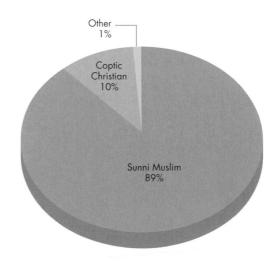

Other
1%

Coptic
Christian
10%

Sunni Muslim
89%

▲ Major religions

particularly among the educated middle class, while in the countryside traditional dress is still common, partly because it is better suited to work in the fields.

Today, 10 per cent of Egyptians are Coptic Christians, followers of a religion that grew out of Christianity and was formally established in the third century AD. Coptic Christianity traces certain of its traditions back to the days of ancient Egypt. For example, feast days called *moulids* hark back to ancient Egyptian festivities. They involve fair-like celebrations at which acrobats, jugglers, dancers and snake charmers perform. The Egyptian constitution guarantees freedom of religious worship, but sometimes Coptic Christians have been targeted by Islamic extremists.

? Did you know?

The head of the Coptic Church, the Patriarch of Alexandria, is spiritual leader of some 50 million Coptic Christians worldwide.

Focus on: Religion in ancient Egypt

Religion played a major role in ancient Egypt. People worshipped many gods and goddesses, who were each responsible for a particular aspect of daily life. Most deities were associated with a particular animal. In Egyptian paintings and sculptures gods are often shown with their animal's head. For example, Anubis, god of the dead, has a jackal's head, while Thoth, god of wisdom, has the head of an ibis (a wading bird). Each town and village had its own protective deity. On feast days, a statue of the god was paraded through the streets, after which celebrations were held with feasting, dancing, juggling and acrobatic displays.

◄ Coptic clergymen tend to an infant during a Mass at Bilyana. Many Coptic Christians believe they face increasing discrimination from Egyptian Muslims because of their faith.

CHAPTER 12

Leisure and Tourism

In ancient Egypt, holidays coincided with religious festivals. Today, Muslim festivals such as Id al-Fitr, which ends Ramadan (the month of fasting), are public holidays, while Coptic Christians celebrate Easter and Christmas.

HOLIDAYS, SPORT AND LEISURE

During religious festivals and vacations, city dwellers with country roots return to their home villages to visit their families. In summer, better-off city dwellers flee the stifling heat to holiday at Mediterranean resorts such as Alexandria. In 2003, some 3.6 million Egyptians travelled abroad as tourists.

The most popular sport in Egypt is football, sometimes played by girls as well as boys. Local and national teams have a big following, with people crowding into cafés with TVs to watch important matches. Basketball, golf, squash, hockey, tennis and swimming, especially long-distance swimming, are also popular. Track and field sports, ball games, rowing and fishing are enjoyed today, as they were in ancient Egypt. Horseracing has an enthusiastic following, and there are racecourses at Cairo and Alexandria.

The most popular leisure activity in Egypt is socializing with members of one's own sex. Men meet at cafés to share news over a cup of strong, sweet coffee or tea, and sometimes a *sheesha*, or water pipe. Board games such as *tawla* (like backgammon), cards and dominoes are played with relish. Traditionally, Egyptian women do not meet at cafés, but at home or in the local park. Today, young middle-class city women may meet at a shopping mall, cinema or fast-food restaurant.

? Did you know?

Egypt's film industry is the largest in Arab world. This has resulted in Egyptian Arabic being the most widely understood form of Arabic.

◄ The bazaar is the centre of daily life in any Egyptian city. Food, spices, leather goods, household utensils, clothes, textiles and craftware can all be bought here.

Egyptians are keen cinemagoers and TV watchers. The film industry dates from the 1920s, and peaked in the 1960s, when an average of one film a day was made! About 100 films are still released each year. The most popular genres are musicals, romantic dramas and historical epics. Youssef Chahine is the best known director. Film stars, such as male lead Adel Imam and belly dancer Fifi Abduh, have a big following.

Since the 1960s, television has overtaken traditional forms of entertainment, such as storytelling. A variety of terrestrial and satellite channels offers a choice of viewing, including soap operas and entertainment shows from Egypt and abroad. *Fawazeer* is a month-long bonanza of TV entertainment during Ramadan. It includes a competition in which viewers must use clues embedded in different programmes to solve a puzzle. Prizes are awarded to winners at the end of the month.

In the last 20 years, Egyptian culture has been affected by the communications revolution. Access to the Internet and to films and TV programmes from the West has given ordinary Egyptians an insight into life there.

FAMILY LIFE

Most Egyptians spend a large part of their leisure time with their families. This is the centre of life in Egypt, whether in wealthy city suburbs, slums or the countryside. Extended families are common, with grandparents, parents and children and even aunts, uncles and cousins under one roof. Egyptians generally dote on their children. Until recently, women tended to look after old people at home, but now more women are going out to work. Also today, some husbands work abroad and families may therefore be split up for months at a time.

▼ Men relax over a game of dominoes in a café in Giza.

FOOD

The staple diet of ordinary Egyptians is bread and *fuul*, broad beans that are boiled or made into a dish called *taamiya*. The most commonly eaten evening meal is vegetable stew mopped up with hunks of bread. Chickpea hummus, rice and kebabs are also popular dishes. The diet is mostly vegetarian, but meat and fish are commonly eaten by middle-class Egyptians. Islam forbids the eating of pork. In cities, Western-style foods such as hamburgers, pasta and pizza are becoming more popular, especially with younger people.

TOURISM

Tourism is one of Egypt's most important industries, and the biggest single source of foreign earnings. The pyramids at Giza are one of the main attractions, bringing visitors from Europe, North America, Japan and elsewhere. Tourists also visit Cairo's Museum of Antiquities, where the treasures from Tutankhamun's tomb are displayed. Many then travel to Luxor to view the temple of Karnak and the Valley of the Kings, and may go on to Aswan to visit the temple of Abu Simbel further south. Increasing numbers of tourists flock to Red Sea resorts, such as Hurghada and Sharm el Sheikh, to enjoy the sunshine and the superb diving around the coral reefs. The rapid growth of Red Sea resorts is causing problems for the environment (see page 55).

Since the 1990s, there has been a marked increase in tourism, with the number of visitors doubling between 1995 and 2003. However, the industry is highly vulnerable to unrest and terrorism in the Middle East. The 1997 Luxor bombings and the 2004 and 2005 attacks at Taba, Nuweiba and Sharm el Sheikh all caused steep drops in tourist numbers, as did the bombing of the World Trade Center in New York on September 11, 2001. These declines harm the Egyptian economy and cause widespread job losses at hotels, shops, restaurants and other facilities that cater for tourists

? Did you know?

The Great Pyramid, standing 137 m (450 ft) high, is built out of 2.3 million blocks of stone.

◀ The rock-cut temples of Abu Simbel (see page 27) were built by the pharaoh, Ramses II. The larger temple, shown here, is flanked by four giant statues of Ramses.

Focus on: The pyramids

Egypt has more than 80 pyramids, but by far the best known are the pyramids at Giza, built around 2,600 BC as memorials to the pharaohs Khufu, Khafre and Menkaura. Nearby, the enigmatic statue of the Sphinx, with a human head and lion's body, is carved from a massive outcropping of soft, limestone rock. The layout of the three main pyramids is now thought to reflect the star cluster of Orion, the constellation of Osiris, god of the afterlife.

▲ Tourists relax in the gardens of a luxury hotel in Giza, with a fine view of the pyramids.

Tourism in Egypt

- 📁 Tourist arrivals, millions: 5.746
- 📁 Earnings from tourism in US$: 4,704,000,000
- 📁 Tourism as % foreign earnings: 23.4
- 📁 Tourist departures, millions: 3.644
- 📁 Expenditure on tourism in US$: 1,464,999,936

Source: World Bank

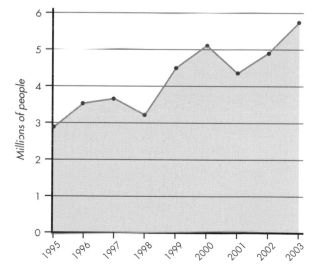

▲ Changes in international tourism, 1995-2003

CHAPTER 13

Environment and Conservation

Egypt's rising population and increasing numbers of tourists are causing damage to the country's fragile environment, with its scant water and fertile land.

POLLUTION

Pollution of the air, water and land are all serious problems in Egypt, particularly in big cities such as Cairo. Levels of lead and dust particles in the capital's air are the highest in the world. Cairo's air is polluted by emissions (waste gases) from vehicles, power plants and factories, and by the burning of crop waste. Between 2000 and 2005, an estimated 10,000 people died each year of respiratory problems. Increased levels of acid in the air, caused by pollution, are eroding Egypt's ancient monuments, including the pyramids and the Sphinx at Giza. The Egyptian Environmental Affairs Agency monitors pollution and is in charge of conservation. Since the 1990s, the agency has taken steps to reduce pollution, including encouraging drivers to convert their vehicles to run on natural gas. Power plants have also converted to gas. Other initiatives include the Cairo Air Improvement Project, which monitors pollution and advises factories to cut their emissions when levels are dangerously high.

In 1999, Egypt produced 0.5 per cent of the world's carbon dioxide emissions. In burning fossil fuels, it contributes to the increase of 'greenhouse gases' that are causing global

▼ A pall of smog hangs over Cairo, causing serious breathing problems for the human population.

warming. Rising sea levels caused by warming oceans threaten to swamp the low-lying Nile Delta, home to millions of people and prime agricultural land. Egypt has signed the Kyoto Protocol, which aims to reduce greenhouse gas emissions, and has made some progress.

Disposing of the huge quantities of waste generated by Cairo's 11 million inhabitants and by domestic animals is a major headache for city authorities. Fortunately, recycling is a major industry in Egypt, where residents of city rubbish tip areas recycle a high percentage of waste.

The waters of the Nile are heavily polluted by chemicals from factories. Fertilizers and pesticides used by farmers also drain into the water, causing harmful algae to multiply. Heavy use by shipping in the Mediterranean, Red Sea and the Suez Canal means that there are regular leaks of oil and other chemicals into the water and occasionally major spills. Around the 1980s, rapid development along Red Sea coasts harmed the region's coral reefs (see box below). Egypt has signed several international treaties that restrict the disposal of waste at sea and in freshwater wetlands. There are also local laws to curb pollution, with fines imposed on companies that break the rules.

Focus on: The Red Sea reefs

Coral reefs in general are the ocean's richest habitat. The reefs of the Red Sea are among the most biodiverse in the world. In the late twentieth century, there was unchecked development along the Red Sea. Long stretches of coast were covered by new resorts, many of which discharged sewage directly into the water. The pollution endangered reef life, including the anemone-like polyps that build the reefs. The anchors of boats dragging along the ocean floor also damaged the coral. Conservation groups realized it was time to take action. Now sewage discharge is carefully regulated, and hotels are charged fees to help pay for conservation. Mooring buoys prevent anchors from damaging diving sites.

◀ An Egyptian woman sifts through rubbish at a dump in Cairo, in search of materials such as clothing that can be recycled and sold.

CONSERVATION

Few creatures can survive in the 95 per cent of Egypt that is desert. Most wildlife is concentrated in and along the Nile and the land next to it. In ancient times, this zone was rich in waterfowl, fish, reptiles and mammals, including lions, elephants, monkeys and gazelle. Many of these species have long since been wiped out as a result of climate change and by hunters. A ban on the hunting of rare species was introduced in 1994.

▼ A diver kneels on a pile of discarded toilets littering the bed of the Red Sea. Waste of many different kinds is harming this marine environment, that until recently was rich in life.

Habitat loss poses a serious threat to Egypt's wildlife. In the twentieth century, the Nile environment was greatly altered. In particular, the Aswan Dam significantly reduced the river's flow, threatening fish and other aquatic life. Now that yearly floods no longer renew the silt of the delta, it is shrinking. Expanding farmlands and urban sprawl are eating into the remaining wild areas. Meanwhile, excessive irrigation of farmland and rapid evaporation have left a high level of mineral salts in the soil, making large areas of farmland unusable.

Since the 1990s, the government has responded to pressure from international conservation groups to 'clean up its act'. In 1992, an environmental

action plan was launched with help from the
World Bank. In 1980, only a tiny fraction of
Egypt was protected by reserves and parks. Today,
Egypt has 26 protected areas, covering 5.7 per cent
of its land area. National parks such as St
Catherine's on the Sinai Peninsula protect
wilderness areas that support mammals such as
jackals and desert foxes. The Ras Mohammed
Marine National Park on the Red Sea protects
coral reefs that are rich in marine life.

? Did you know?

Many species of birds, including storks, cranes,
eagles and songbirds, use the Nile as a 'flyway'
or migration route as they make their seasonal
journeys between Europe and southern Africa.

▶ An Egyptian fruit bat hangs from a tree branch.
These night-active animals are regarded as pests
when they feed on fruit in plantations, but they also
help plants to reproduce by spreading their pollen.

Environmental and conservation data

📂 Forested area as % total land area: 0.2
📂 Protected area as % total land area: 5.7
📂 Number of protected areas: 26

SPECIES DIVERSITY

Category	Known species	Threatened species
Mammals	98	13
Breeding birds	123	7
Reptiles	108	6
Amphibians	11	n/a
Fish	284	n/a
Plants	2,076	2

Source: World Resources Institute

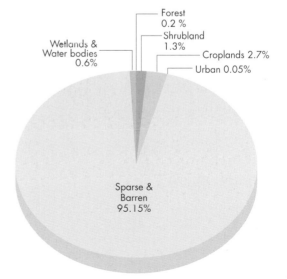

▲ Habitat types as percentage of total area

CHAPTER 14

Future Challenges

Egypt is a developing economy with a large workforce and some important natural resources. In years to come, the government will persist in tackling the difficult problems it faces, including poverty, unemployment and environmental concerns.

In future decades, Egypt will continue to benefit from its strategic geographical position. Egypt's role as a negotiator in the Arab region looks set to continue. This role yields financial benefits in the form of relief from foreign debt. At home, inflation, poverty and overcrowding in cities remain thorny issues. The government will continue to grapple with Islamic fundamentalist groups such as the Muslim Brotherhood and acts of terrorism, which threaten the nation's security and also its lucrative tourist industry. The 2005 election was widely seen as a first step toward full democracy – whetting the public's appetite for a truly democratic and more open political process in Egypt.

Since the 1960s, Egypt has made considerable improvements to health, education and infrastructure, largely with the help of foreign aid. It has tried to foster economic growth and attract foreign investment through economic reforms. However, unrest in the Middle East and Egyptian bureaucracy present obstacles to foreign investors. Increased trade with other Arab nations may help Egypt to boost its

▼ Traffic nears gridlock in the centre of Cairo. Slow-moving vehicles add to the pollution. The construction of new cities has helped to relieve overcrowding in the capital.

exports and reduce its trade deficit. Meanwhile, continued emphasis on birth control will help to ensure reasonable living standards among future generations. However, the Egyptian government faces opposition on this issue from religious fundamentalists.

In years to come, Egypt will continue to rely on assets such as the Suez Canal and its ancient monuments. The tourist industry is likely to expand further, despite terrorism and unrest. Oil and, particularly, natural gas will provide a major source of foreign income, but these industries do little to reduce unemployment or raise general living standards. Egypt's greatest challenge is to exploit its natural resources, such as minerals, and to make the best use of its large workforce. At the same time, the country needs to protect and prevent further damage to its natural environments.

Focus on: South Valley irrigation scheme

The South Valley Development Project is the latest in a long line of large-scale projects to improve Egypt's infrastructure with funds from foreign backers. This highly ambitious scheme involves the construction of a 300-km (185-mile) canal from Lake Nasser to irrigate the desert around the oasis of Baris, to create new farmlands. The first stage of the plan, which involved construction of the shorter Sheikh Zayed Canal and the large Tushka Pumping Station on Lake Nasser, has already been completed. Eventually it is hoped that water pumped from the lake will transform 4,000 hectares of desert into cropland, but the scheme has become controversial because of rising costs that some consider to be a waste of money.

◀ A mosque in Sixth of October City, one of the new generation of cities that have been constructed since the 1970s. However, many Egyptians are reluctant to move far into the desert to locations like this.

Timeline

c. 5,000 BC Egyptian civilization begins along the River Nile. The history of ancient Egypt is divided into the Old, Middle and New Kingdoms, three eras during which powerful dynasties rule.

c. 3,200 BC The kingdoms of Upper and Lower Egypt are united by a pharaoh called Menes.

670 BC Egypt is conquered by the Assyrians.

340-332 BC Persians rule Egypt.

332-30 BC Greek general Alexander conquers Egypt and founds Alexandria. A Greek dynasty rules until 30 BC.

30 BC-AD 324 Romans rule Egypt.

AD 324-639 Egypt is ruled by the Byzantine Empire, based in Constantinople (Istanbul).

639 Egypt is conquered by Arab Muslims. Arab dynasties rule Egypt for much of the next six centuries, except for a period of Turkish rule between 868-969.

969-1171 The Fatimid dynasty rules Egypt.

970 Al-Azhar mosque and Islamic university are founded.

1168 Egypt is invaded by Crusaders (Christian forces) during the wars of the Crusades. The Fatimids ask the Muslim general Saladin to oust the Crusaders.

1171 Saladin ousts the Crusaders, but overthrows the Fatimids. His dynasty, the Ayyubids, rules Egypt until 1250.

1250 A Muslim military caste, the Mamelukes, take control of Egypt.

1517 Ottoman Turks conquer Egypt, but the Mamelukes continue to wield power.

1798 Napoleon Bonaparte briefly conquers Egypt.

1801 Ottoman and British troops oust French troops from Egypt.

1805 An Ottoman officer, Muhammad Ali Pasha, becomes ruler of Egypt. His dynasty rules for 150 years.

1822 French scholar Jean François Champollion succeeds in deciphering the script of ancient Egypt, providing a key to Egypt's past.

1851 Work begins on the Suez Canal, which opens in 1869.

1875 Egypt sells its shares in the Suez Canal to Britain.

1882 Britain seizes control of Egypt to protect its interests in the Suez Canal. The British control the administration of Egypt although the Ottoman khedives (viceroys) continue to rule.

1914 Britain tightens its grip on Egypt by making it into a protectorate (protected country) at the start of the First World War.

1922 Britain grants partial independence to Egypt, but British troops remain.

1936 A new treaty strengthens Egypt's independence, but British troops are still stationed at Suez.

1940-42 Allied and German/Italian troops clash in the region of Suez during the Second World War.

1945 Egypt becomes a founder member of the Arab League and also of the United Nations.

1948-9 Egypt and other Arab nations wage war on the newly created state of Israel, but are defeated.

1952-3 A military coup led by the Free Officers including Gamal Abdel Nasser overthrows the monarchy. Egypt becomes a republic.

1954 Gamal Abdel Nasser becomes ruler of Egypt.

1956 Nasser seizes control of the Suez Canal. Israel, France and Britain invade Egypt but the United Nations ends the fighting.

1958 Egypt, Syria and Yemen form the United Arab States, a union which lasts until 1961.

1960-68 Aswan High Dam is built with the help of Soviet funds and engineers.

1967 Israel is victorious over Arab forces in the Six-Day War. Israel occupies the Sinai Peninsula, the Gaza Strip and other Arab territory.

1970 Anwar el-Sadat becomes president following Nasser's death.

1973 The Yom Kippur War. Egypt and Syria launch an attack on Israel and reoccupy the Sinai Peninsula before US and Soviet forces intervene to establish a ceasefire.

1977 Sadat makes a historic speech at the Israeli parliament, the Knesset, brokering peace with Israel.

1978 National Democratic Party is founded in Egypt. Sadat signs a peace treaty, the Camp David Accords, with Israel in exchange for the Sinai Peninsula.

1979 Egypt is expelled from the Arab League.

1980-81 Sadat pursues an 'open door' policy, seeking alliance and financial help from the West.

1981 Hosni Mubarak becomes Egyptian president following the assassination of Sadat.

1980-88 Egypt supports Iraq during the war between Iraq and Iran.

1989 Egypt is re-admitted to the Arab League.

1990-1 Egypt opposes Iraq's seizure of Kuwait, and helps UN forces defeat Iraq in the Persian Gulf War.

1992 A major earthquake strikes Cairo, causing more than 560 deaths. Egypt launches an Environmental Action Plan as recommended by the World Bank.

1997 Islamic terrorist group, Al-Gama'a al-Islamiya, massacres 58 tourists and four Egyptians in Luxor.

2000 Egyptian government tries to crush Islamic extremists by making mass arrests.

2002 Egyptian pound is devalued, which leads to inflation.

2004 Al-Gama'a al-Islamiya launches attacks on tourists in the cities of Taba and Nuweiba. Egypt's government carries out a programme of economic reforms.

July 2005 A triple bombing at the Red Sea resort of Sharm el Sheikh kills 63 people.

September 2005 Hosni Mubarak is elected to a fifth term as president, following a more open election.

April 2006 Suicide bombers kill 23 people at Dahab.

Glossary

Abdicate When a ruler gives up the throne.

Acid rain Rain which is slightly acidic because it has been polluted by waste gases from car exhausts and power stations.

Allegory A type of writing in which meaning is expressed indirectly, through a story or fable.

Allied forces During the Second World War, the name given to the combined forces of Britain, France, the USA and the Soviet Union opposing Germany, Italy and Japan.

Arable land Land on which crops can be grown.

Biodiverse Having a wide range of living species.

Caste A hereditary class within a society.

Catamaran A double-hulled sailing boat.

Civil service The administrative body involved in running a country.

Cold War The period following the Second World War, between 1945 and 1991, during which the Soviet Union and its allies and the USA and its allies were very hostile and mistrustful of one another. Egypt was courted by both sides during this era, because of its strategic position in the Middle East.

Compensate To give a person, institution or a country payment in recognition that a wrong has been done.

Constitution A set of laws governing a country or organization.

Controversial An issue that provokes debate.

Coup A violent or non-democratic change of government.

Deity A god or goddess.

Delta A low-lying, marshy area at a river's mouth, formed of sediment dropped by the river as it reaches the sea.

Democracy A political system in which members of parliament are chosen by people voting in free elections.

Depose To overthrow a ruler.

Developed countries The richer countries of the world, whose industries are well-developed, including the USA, UK, Germany and Japan.

Developing countries The poorer countries of the world, whose industries are less well-developed, such as many African nations.

Dictator A ruler with absolute (complete) authority.

Dynasty A ruling family, in which power passes from the ruler to his (or, more rarely, her) heir.

Erosion The wearing away of the land by natural forces such as wind, rain and ice. Erosion is sometimes increased by deforestation or overgrazing by animals.

Ethnic Classification of people according to their racial origins.

Flash flood A flood that occurs after heavy rain.

Fossil fuel Coal, oil, gas and other fuels formed from fossilized remains of plants or animals that lived and died millions of years ago.

Global warming Rising temperatures worldwide, caused by the increase of carbon dioxide and other gases in the atmosphere that trap the sun's heat.

Gross Domestic Product The total value of all the goods and services produced by a country in a year.

Inflation A general increase in prices within a country.

Infrastructure The basic facilities needed for a country to function, including electricity, communications and transport.

Irrigate To water the land in order to grow crops.

Islam The Muslim faith, a major world religion based on the teachings of the Prophet Mohammed as recorded in the Koran.

Islamic fundamentalist A Muslim who wishes strict Islamic law to be imposed.

Isthmus A narrow strip of land with sea on either side, linking two larger pieces of land.

Khedive The title given to the Ottoman (Turkish) rulers of Egypt.

Legislative Relating to law and law-making.

Literacy The ability to read and write.

Nationalize When a company or institution is taken under state ownership and control.

Nomad A person who spends his or her life moving from place to place.

Oasis A fertile place in a desert, supplied by underground water.

Phonetic Relating to speech sounds.

Protectorate A country that is under the protection and thus the control of another.

Recycling The process of reclaiming useful materials from waste so that they can be used again.

Referendum A public vote on a single issue.

Renewable energy Energy which comes from sources that will not run out, such as the sun, wind and flowing water.

Republic A nation state without a monarch, ruled by the people or their representatives.

Silt Fine sand or clay carried by river water and deposited as sediment.

Subsistence farming A type of agriculture in which farmers grow food for their own needs, with little left over to sell for profit.

Tectonic plate One of the giant rigid sections that make up the earth's outer layer, or crust.

United Nations (UN) An organization founded at the end of the Second World War with the aim of preventing future wars.

Further Information

BOOKS TO READ

AA Explorer: Egypt
(AA Publishing, regularly updated)

The Changing Face of Egypt
Ron Ragsdale
(Hodder Wayland, 2002)

Country Fact Files: Egypt
Emma Loveridge
(Macdonald Young Books, 1997)

Countries of the World: Egypt
John Pallister
(Evans Brothers, 2004)

Eyewitness Guides: Pyramid
James Putnam
(Dorling Kindersley, 2002)

Encyclopedia of Ancient Egypt
(Usborne Publishing Ltd, 2004)

Horrible Histories: The Awesome Egyptians
Terry Deary, Martin Brown (illustrator)
(Scholastic Hippo, 1993)

Insight Guide: Egypt
(Insight Guides, regularly updated)

Letters From Around the World: Egypt
David Cumming
(Cherrytree Books, 2005)

Picture the Past: Life in an Egyptian Workers' Village
Jane Shuter
(Heinemann Library, 2005)

River Journey: The Nile
Rob Bowden
(Hodder Children's Books, 2003)

FICTION

The Cairo Trilogy: Palace Walk, Palace of Desire and *Sugar Street*
Naguib Mahfouz
(Everyman's Library, 2001)

Tales of Ancient Egypt
Roger Lancelyn Green, Heather Copley (illustrator)
(Puffin Books, 1995)

USEFUL WEBSITES

http://www.sis.gov.eg
The Egyptian government site, with a wide range of information about aspects of the country.

www.touregypt.net
Official site of the Egyptian Tourist Board, with details of antiquities, national parks and a range of other tourist attractions.

http://news.bbc.co.uk/1/hi/world/middle_east/country_profiles/737642.stm
BBC news country profile on Egypt.

www.cia.gov/cia/publications/factbook/geos/eg.html
The CIA World Factbook, providing up-to-date statistics on Egypt.

http://www.worldinfozone.com/country.php?country=Egypt
Information about Egypt's geography, economy, government and people.

Index

Page numbers in **bold** indicate pictures.

About the Author

Dr Jen Green received a doctorate from the University of Sussex (Department of English and American Studies) in 1982. She worked in publishing for fifteen years and is now a full-time writer who has written more than 150 books for children. She lives in Sussex.